MANIFEST EVERYTHING
A CHEATSHEET FOR HAVING YOUR VERSION OF "IT ALL"

JENNIFER BLANCHARD

CONTENTS

Introduction vii

PART ONE
THE METHODOLOGY

M = Massive clarity 5
A = Advance gratitude 11
N = Now decide you're worthy 19
I = Inner work 23
F = Feel it 26
E = Embody it 30
S = Show up for your life 34
T = Take inspired action 37
A Manifest Method Example 41
The Manifest Method Cheatsheet 51

PART TWO
THE WORKBOOK

MANIFEST Anything 55

The Manifesting Trifecta: 91
The MANIFEST Everything Crash Course 95
Please Leave A Review On Amazon 97
Acknowledgments 99
About the Author 101

© Copyright 2023 Jennifer Blanchard

All Rights Reserved

No part of this book may be reproduced or used in any manner without the prior written permission of the copyright owner, except for the use of brief quotations in a book review.

To request permission, contact the publisher: support@jenniferblanchard.net

Author Jennifer Blanchard
P.O. Box 245
Le Roy, NY 14482
www.dreamlifeorbust.com

Disclaimer

The information in this book is meant for educational and entertainment purposes only. The author and publisher make no guarantees concerning the results or the level of success you may experience by following the advice and strategies contained in this book, and you accept the risk that results will differ for each individual. The stories and examples provided in this book show exceptional results, and are not intended to represent or guarantee that you will achieve the same or similar results, now or in the future.

The author and the publisher assume no responsibility for your actions or decisions, and hereby specifically disclaim any responsibility to any party for any liability, loss, risk, damage, or disruption of any kind caused by direct or indirect use and application of any of the contents of this book.

This book is not intended to be a substitute for legal, medical, psychological, accounting, or financial advice, or for direct expert assistance. If such level of assistance is required, the services of a competent professional should be sought. The use of this book implies your acceptance of this disclaimer.

*This book is dedicated to my
A Course In Miracles Reverend and friend, Barbara Adams*

INTRODUCTION

I honestly wasn't going to write this book. I've already written two very in-depth books on manifesting (you may have read them—*F*ck the How* and *Quantum Leap Your Life*). I didn't think I had anything else to say. But it turns out, I did. Learning to manifest intentionally is a lifelong journey. And the better I've gotten at embodying my process, the clearer I am that I need to continue teaching and writing about it.

I didn't want this book to be just another repeat of my previous two manifesting books (which is why I avoided writing it for so long). But I did feel called to share the refined version of the manifesting process that I talk about in my book, *F*ck the How*. That process is still great and works just as well, but the version I'm sharing in this book changes everything.

I wrote this book as a short-and-sweet cheatsheet on manifesting, covering everything you need to know to manifest whatever you want now and forevermore, but without diving too deep. If you want a deep dive, that's what my other

INTRODUCTION

two manifesting books are for (I call this *the Manifesting Trifecta*—you can read more about it at the end of this book).

I wanted this book to be a reference you can return to over and over again, and I also wanted it to be a place where you could dig in and work through the methodology I'm presenting here. So I've split this book into two parts.

Part One is The Methodology. In this part, I'll be going over the eight steps in the Manifest Method. I'll then give you a list of what to read in *F*ck the How* and/or *Quantum Leap Your Life* if you want to go deeper into the concepts from each chapter in this book. I'll also share one specific example that uses the eight steps, so you can see a real manifestation come to life from initial thought to physical form.

Part Two is The Workbook. In this part, you will work through each step in the Manifest Method with specific questions to ask yourself, additional things to consider, and possible actions to take.

My intention is for you to read Part One and then dive into Part Two and use the workbook to help you implement the Manifest Method in your life and start to see results. The more you use this method to manifest things, the more you'll embody the process until it becomes a part of who you are. Then you'll be able to go through the eight steps naturally, without having to write it down in a workbook (unless you want to!).

I can't wait to see what you manifest in your life! If you feel like sharing, join my free Facebook group, The Feel-Good Life Club: www.facebook.com/groups/feelgoodlifecenter.

Now let's do this thing!

Dream life or bust,

jennifer

INTRODUCTION

P.S. I use the term "the Universe" to refer to the higher power often called God or Source Energy by others, as that is the term that resonates most for me. But I may also use these terms interchangeably throughout this book because I consider them to be the same thing.

PART ONE
THE METHODOLOGY

There's a major misconception about manifesting that I want to clear up right now. Manifestation isn't something you have to learn how to do. You're already doing it, and you have been since the day you were born. Your thoughts, beliefs, feelings, and actions have been co-creating things with the Universe your entire life. The problem is, the majority of people still don't know this, so they're manifesting unconsciously (meaning they don't know they're doing it). Lack of awareness puts you at a disadvantage because then you're not being intentional with your manifesting, you're just magnetizing to yourself and your life whatever your dominant subconscious thoughts, beliefs, and feelings are.

For most of us, those dominant subconscious thoughts, beliefs, and feelings are negative, limiting, and don't align with us having what we want. And that's why there are so many people teaching about manifestation now. Because being aware that you're manifesting and having a process to do it intentionally is beneficial not only to yourself but also to the ripple effect you create in the world.

When I manifested the love of my life four years ago, I was able to look back in hindsight and see that I had my own specific manifestation process. It was a refined version of the process I wrote about in my book, *F*ck the How*, and it gave me even more clarity on how to manifest whatever I want.

For fun and to make it more memorable, I turned the eight steps into a methodology with an acronym that spells out MANIFEST. Each letter represents a step in the process.

Here's what the methodology looks like (each step will be explained in the coming chapters):

M - *Massive clarity*—When you know what you want, it's easier to manifest it.
A - *Advance gratitude*—Being grateful in advance helps you become magnetic to the things you desire to have.
N - *Now decide you're worthy*—Feeling unworthy is one of the top reasons you don't get what you want.
I - *Inner work*—Doing the work on the inside to change your mindset, thoughts, beliefs, and feelings is foundational to the rest of the process.
F - *Feel it*—Create inside yourself the feelings of already having the thing you want.
E - *Embody it*—Take on the identity of the version of you who already has it.
S - *Show up for your life*—Live your life and let all the things you want (or the how for getting them) come to you.
T - *Take inspired action*—When you feel inspired to take an

action or get an inner nudge to do something or go somewhere or say something to someone about something, DO IT!

I now intentionally apply this same process to everything in my life, and I have begun manifesting a whole lot more of what I want, and much faster and more often than ever before. I've used it to manifest everything from love to increased book royalties to the Jeep I wanted and everything in between.

In this part of the book, I'll be diving into the specifics around each step of this process, including all of the micro-steps within each step, so you'll have what you need to use it in your own life.

The first time I talked about the Manifest Method on my @fuckthehow TikTok channel, the video got tens of thousands of views, and someone even commented and said that it was *"about a hundred books and thousands of dollars in manifesting courses distilled down into the best process flow I've ever heard."*

That's how I roll. I like to keep it simple and make it easy to implement and use in your actual real life to get the things you want (and more). I'm concise and I remove the fluff. It's just my style. This book is the same.

I'm giving you everything you need to know to use the Manifest Method really well in your life, and nothing more. If you want a deeper dive into any or all of the concepts discussed in this book, definitely read my books, *F*ck the How* and *Quantum Leap Your Life*.

I've done my best to separate the steps in this book, but just keep in mind they all work together and so there may be some crossover. This is a good thing. As you apply the Manifest Method in your own life, you'll start to notice there are certain manifestations where you can do some or all of the steps easily and quickly and other ones where you may need to dig in to shift something. The steps working together will help you get faster results the more you practice using the process.

The goal is to get you using the Manifest Method automatically, so you don't have to think too much about it, and it just becomes a part of who you are and how you live your life.

M = MASSIVE CLARITY
AKA DECIDE WHAT YOU WANT, EITHER SPECIFICALLY OR IN GENERAL

This is always the starting point in every manifestation process. You have to be clear on what you want. That clarity can look one of three ways:

- Know what you want specifically
- Know what you want in general
- A combination of the two—know what you want in general and what your non-negotiable specifics are (this is what I prefer most of the time when I'm manifesting)

The most important factor in deciding what you want is understanding where your current belief level is at—**Do you fully, one hundred percent believe you can have the thing you want?**

Close your eyes and take a slow, deep breath in for five seconds. Hold it for five seconds. Slowly breathe out for five seconds. Repeat at least two more times.

Now put your hand on your heart and ask yourself: **On a scale of one to ten** (with ten being full one hundred percent belief and one being no belief at all), **how much do I believe I will get to have [insert the thing you want]?**

The first number that pops into your mind will let you know where you're at, belief-wise.

If your number is an eight or higher, you're good to go. If your number is hanging out in the middle, you could still choose to go with that thing or do what I'm about to suggest for when the number is low.

And if your number is lower than a three, there are a couple of things you can do:

- Increase your belief level
- Be more general with what you want

Being general with what you're manifesting is the best way to decrease any resistance you may feel to believing you can have the exact thing you want. It also gives the Universe more space to work within (specifics really limit your options).

For example, instead of deciding you only want to be with this one specific guy that you dated for a few months before it ended, decide you want to manifest the love of your life in general. That guy you dated for a few months may come back into your life and be the one for you, or you might meet someone you don't even know about yet. Being general leaves space for magic and miracles.

IF YOU WANT TO INCREASE YOUR BELIEF LEVEL

Sometimes there's something specific—or something that has certain specifics—that you just really, really want. No matter what, it has to be that thing. In this case, your only option is to increase your belief level.

You need to find a way to wrap your head around you having the exact thing you want and being able to handle it (and not self-sabotage when it shows up).

Here are some ways for you to do that:

- **Work on reprogramming any limiting beliefs or thoughts** that tell you that you can't have what you want
- **Find evidence to prove it to yourself**—Look for someone who has what you want that you can relate to in some way (ex: you have a similar backstory, you're both from the same hometown, you both have degrees from the same college, you both have brown hair, etc.)

Both of those things will help you to increase your belief level. Once you increase it, you'll be more open and receptive, which will help you to receive what you want.

Meeting a self-published author who had the same backstory as me and who had written a bestseller on Amazon was all the evidence I needed to shoot my belief level through the roof. And four months later, I also became a bestselling author on Amazon.

IF YOU DON'T KNOW WHAT YOU WANT

This is probably the number one question I get asked by my clients, students, and online community—*But what if I don't know what I want?* And my answer is always the same thing: **you do know, but you're just not admitting it to yourself yet.**

That may be a harsh response, but I believe in helping people to stand in their power. There's nothing powerful about thinking you don't know what your own desires are.

Maybe you're not giving yourself permission to want what you actually want. Maybe you haven't allowed yourself to even consider what you want because you don't believe you can have it. Maybe your lack of knowing *how* it will happen is making you not want it. Or maybe you're just too scared to say it out loud. But deep down in your heart of hearts, you know what you want.

For clarity purposes, here are some things to consider:

- **What triggers you?** A "trigger" is something that causes a strong negative emotional reaction in you. Sometimes the things that trigger us are worth looking into.
- **Who or what do you resent and why?** A lot of the time resentments are just hidden desires that we don't believe are possible for us.
- **What makes you feel jealous or FOMO (fear of missing out)?** Again, it's worth exploring 'cause hidden desires could be lurking below the surface.
- **What do you dislike about your life right now?** Contrast is always a good place to look for your

true desires.
- **If you could go back, start over, and recreate your life knowing everything that you now know, what would you want?**

THE THING VS. THE NOW THING

One final thing to check in on is whether what you want is the Thing or the Now Thing. Let me explain. The Thing is part of the long-term vision you have for your life overall or a specific area of your life. It's something you want, but it doesn't feel like a desire you need to fulfill right now. It's something you know you'll eventually feel a burning desire for, but right now you're good. You're okay with it not being in your life at this time.

Whereas the Now Thing is the desire you feel a yearning for right now. You want it. You need it. It has to be now.

The things you feel a deep, burning desire for are the things that will often manifest fastest because true desire is such a strong emotion and energy. It will make you step out of your comfort zone in ways you never thought you would. A burning desire can even override any doubts or limiting beliefs that would typically get in your way.

And this is why it matters whether or not you give yourself permission to want (and have) what you really want. Not what you think you should want. Not what someone else wants for you. But what you really and truly actually desire for yourself.

I believe our desires are given to us by the Universe because it's something the Universe wants to experience through us. You are meant to have, do, and be the things you desire and dream of. You're made for it, created for it, and you have what it takes. And the Universe wants it for you.

INTEND IT AND DECIDE

There's something to be said about intention and deciding. If you often don't get the things you want, it's not because they're not available to you or because they're not possible for you. Likely, you haven't actually decided to have them yet.

You've been thinking about it and dreaming about it, but you haven't yet made the decision and then moved forward from that decision consistently. But you can choose to do that now. It all starts with deciding.

Set a powerful intention for yourself and your life. Decide you're going to have the things you want, and then back that decision up every moment of every day with your thoughts, beliefs, feelings, and actions. Over and over and over again. Entertain nothing less. This is how you help the Universe move mountains for you.

REFERENCE THIS

If you want to go deeper into the concepts from this chapter, read the following:

In *F*ck the How*:
• Chapter 2: Get Clear On What You Want

In *Quantum Leap Your Life*:
• Chapter One: Quantum Leaping

A = ADVANCE GRATITUDE
AKA BE GRATEFUL FOR WHAT YOU WANT IN ADVANCE OF HAVING IT

You have to be grateful for the things you want before you have them. This isn't something you haven't heard before. Gratitude is the pinnacle of manifestation. It's the thing every manifestation and mindset guru and book teaches. I'm also going to tell you about being grateful. However, the way I'm going to explain it might be different than you've ever heard before.

This is a manifesting nuance that I didn't yet fully understand when I wrote my book, *F*ck the How*. This nuance is small, but it's powerful.

I used to teach—and it's also taught by many other manifestation teachers—that you have to ask the Universe for what you want. First, get clear on what you want, and then ask for it. (I even co-wrote a book called *Miraclefesting* where we talked about manifestation in three steps: Ask, Believe, Receive.)

But here's the truth: you don't need to ask. You never have to ask. Or at least, not in the way you probably think you do.

The Universe isn't a being you have to get permission from

like you did when you were a kid with your parents or guardian. It's also not "above you" looking down and judging you and deciding if it will grant you what you're asking for. The Universe is an energy that you can choose to intentionally co-create with. It's on your side. It wants what you want.

As I mentioned, the Universe gave you your dreams and desires because it's something that it wants to experience through you specifically. And for that reason, the "permission" is already given. It's inherent. It comes along with the dream or desire.

This means the only permission that's actually needed is permission from yourself to yourself. Permission to have what you want. Permission to dream big (or bigger). Permission to create and live the life that only you can.

Sometimes you don't even realize you haven't given yourself permission because it's happening unconsciously. So now that you're aware of it, be super real and check in with yourself: *What do you want, and have you given yourself full permission to have it?*

WHAT TO DO INSTEAD OF ASK

Here's where gratitude comes in. Or at least, a part of it. There's also a part where you're thankful for what you already have, but we'll get to that in a coming chapter. Right now, let's talk about how to use gratitude in place of asking.

Since your dreams and desires come from the Universe, and the Universe is on your side, wants what you want, and permission comes along with it, all you have to do is be grateful. Gratitude in advance of having what you want magnetizes it to you.

Instead of asking, say thank you.

So I will say something (usually out loud), such as, *"Thank you Universe for getting me a front-row parking space at the grocery store today."* I will say this as I'm on my way driving to the store. Or I'll say, *"Thank you for finding my missing ring and leading me to it."* I'll often say this when I don't know where something is and don't feel like looking for it. Or I might say, *"Thank you for finding the perfect people to enroll in my course and magnetizing them to it."* I always say things like this when I'm launching something in my business. For extra oomph I'll then add, *"And so it is."*

I consider gratitude in advance to be equivalent to praying. I pray all the time, just not how I was taught to by my religious upbringing. I don't ask to be granted things. I don't beg or plead for help and then hope for the best.

I pray by having gratitude in advance for whatever I want. I now know asking isn't required, and by asking, you automatically come from a place of lack. You can't receive what you want from a place of not having it. You must be grateful in advance for it, from a place of knowing it's already yours.

It's almost like setting an intention and making a decision all rolled into one. My belief is that the Universe wants to help me and guide me and figure things out for me. That's what co-creativity is, creating something in cooperation with someone/something else. And because I believe this so deeply, and have tested it out enough times, I trust that it will work and what I want (or something even better) will show up for me.

BE GRATEFUL AND THEN SURRENDER IT

Once you've stated your gratitude in advance, you have to let it go and surrender your desire. Of course, this is much easier said than done. We tend to be very attached to the things we want, especially the stuff that feels "big" to us. We mistakenly think we have to hold on tight or we might not get it. None of which is conducive to having what you want show up.

The more you cling to something, the more you make it want to run from you. Neediness, whininess, and desperation are all repellant energies.

Surrender comes from a place of trust. A place of feeling good enough where you're at while also knowing fully that you get to have more. A place of truly believing the Universe wants to help you.

Trust in the Universe doesn't happen overnight, especially if you were raised in an unaligned religious upbringing or have had any kind of God trauma in your life. That's why I recommend starting with something that you see as "small." A front-row parking space. Locating something you misplaced. Finding a dollar on the ground. Whatever you feel like you can believe in enough to not worry about it.

The Universe can and will move mountains for you, but you have to first believe those mountains are movable.

The biggest reason most people can't surrender fully is because they don't know how something will happen or come about. And because they can't see how they also can't get themselves to believe it's possible for them or that it will actually happen. Surrender feels impossible coming from that place.

But when you want something and you're able to trust and

know that when you're grateful in advance it is given, surrender happens naturally.

At this point in my journey, surrender is so easy for me with most things because I no longer care to worry about anything. I no longer want to figure things out myself. I no longer desire to work hard to make things happen. And I know I don't have to. That was just stuff I was taught, but that doesn't make it true. I get to choose. And I choose surrender.

THE HOW IS NOT ON YOU

I wrote an entire book on this, so I won't go into it too much here, but I've said it before and I'll say it forever: *the how is not on you*. You don't have to know how. You don't have to figure out how. The how is not your job.

Your job is to be clear on what you want, be grateful in advance, and follow the rest of the steps I'm going to talk about. Figuring out the how is not one of those steps. The how is the Universe's job.

You feel the dream or desire, you say thank you to the Universe for making it happen or figuring it out, and then you get to go about living your life while the Universe does the work of aligning, rearranging, and setting things up.

What a relief! It's a breath of fresh air to finally accept that you don't have to do anything all on your own. The Universe is always there and available and willing, so long as you willingly engage with it.

RETURN TO THE FOUR TRUTHS OF SURRENDER

I share these four truths in all of my books on manifesting. These truths are what allowed me to feel confident surrendering the outcome of my marriage to the Universe, which resulted in me manifesting a divorce and changing my entire life for the better. I call them truths, but they're simply beliefs I have chosen to take on as truths. They are true for me because I believe them to be so.

To take these truths on for yourself, just decide they're true. Don't allow yourself to question or think twice about it.

The Four Truths of Surrender are:

1. The Universe is on it the moment you have gratitude in advance for it.
2. It's working, even if you can't see it with your physical senses yet (especially when you can't).
3. It's working better than you can ever imagine.
4. For every one step you take, the Universe takes more.

When you've been grateful in advance for something and then surrendered, but you still catch yourself worrying about it, you have two options: say thank you again for it already showing up, or go back and reread the Four Truths of Surrender. Remind yourself of how this thing really works. And then get your head back in the game.

Because that's what it actually is, you know? A game between yourself and the Universe to see how much you're willing to allow yourself to have, how fast you're willing to believe, and how deep you're willing to surrender. Your free will controls all of it. You could have a million dollars tomorrow if you truly believed you could. It's your belief that stops you from getting it (and your belief is tainted by things like rules you've been taught, past experiences, societal expectations around what it takes to make a million dollars, etc.). We'll talk about beliefs soon.

THIS OR SOMETHING BETTER

A major part of surrender is not just releasing the how of getting what you want, but also the surrender of the actual thing you want as well. Yes, you get to have what you want. And when you do receive it, you'll be so excited and grateful for what showed up.

But sometimes, it may look a little different than what you thought it might look like. This is something to make peace with for yourself.

Sometimes you have a vision for what you want, and you receive that exact thing. Other times, you get something that matches the in-general of everything you want, it just looks a little different than you expected it to. This happens because you have a limited vantage point by which to view the world. You can only see, believe, and imagine it to a certain point. Beyond that, it eludes you.

You may think this one specific guy is the one you're supposed to be with. Be grateful in advance for him and for having the relationship and love you desire, in general. The Universe will send you the exact match to everything you've ever dreamed of in a person, partner, lover, and friend. But it may not come in the package of that specific guy you thought it would be.

That's what "this or something better" means. Know what you want but stay open-minded. Trust that the Universe's all-knowing vantage point is actually better than your limited one, and trust that whatever does show up is right when it feels right.

REFERENCE THIS

If you want to go deeper into the concepts from this chapter, read the following:

In *F*ck the How*:
- Chapter 3: Surrender It To the Universe

N = NOW DECIDE YOU'RE WORTHY
AKA DECIDE TO SEE YOURSELF AS WORTHY, DESERVING, AND GOOD ENOUGH

Worthiness is a decision. It really is that simple. But we overcomplicate it because we've been taught so much nonsense about needing to earn worthiness and pay dues to be good enough.

None of that is true, by the way. It's simply a collection of limiting beliefs that were passed down from one generation to the next and then taken on as truth. It's no one's fault. Whoever taught this stuff to you was only teaching you based on what they learned and their life experience with it. And they were coming from a good place and doing the best they could. There's no reason to blame your past, but plenty of reasons to recreate your future.

And that's why step three of the Manifest Method is to now decide you're worthy. Without this critical step, it's unlikely that you will get what you want. You must first believe and see yourself as worthy, deserving, and good enough to have it.

DECIDE THAT YOUR WORTH IS NO LONGER IN QUESTION

You were born worthy and there's nothing you can do to change that. You've always been worthy. You will always be worthy. You're still worthy, even when you feel less than so. You may question it at times, but that doesn't erase your inherent value. You are a divine child of the Universe. Created in the likeness of the Creator. You have the same energy and power inside of you that created everything that exists, and you can use it to co-create your life exactly as you desire it to be.

You are worthy. You are deserving. You are good enough. Always. Now and forevermore.

Decide that you will no longer question your worthiness. It's not a question to be answered, it's a statement to be made over and over again: *I am worthy.*

RELEASE AND REPROGRAM ANYTHING THAT DOESN'T MATCH

Deciding to know you're worthy may require you to also release and reprogram any old thoughts, beliefs, or old memories that don't match that decision.

This means being honest with yourself and taking a good look at what you have going on internally. Your thoughts, beliefs, feelings, memories, stories, or anything that makes you feel bad are good things to start with.

Once you change your internal state, that's when you'll see changes on the outside. Your internal state (conscious and subconscious) creates your external reality. It's all a mirror. So at any given time, you can know what's going on inside of you regarding any area of your life by looking at what's been showing up in that area.

REMOVE, REPLACE, OR SHIFT ANYTHING THAT MAKES YOU FEEL NOT GOOD ENOUGH

You may not even realize it, but you could be surrounded by things that subtly send you the message that you're not good enough. If you look around at your house, your closet, your car, or your life, you may see things that, when you really stop to think about it, make you feel not enough. Things like old stained t-shirts or clothes that no longer fit you still hanging in your closet, or a boss that constantly berates you, or just the way you talk to yourself on the daily can all add up to making you feel not good enough.

These are the things to either remove from your life and replace with something else. If you can't remove or replace certain things, then find a way to shift your perspective or belief about it or what it means for you.

SHIFT IN THE MOMENT

You also want to practice being aware of your thoughts and feelings in the moment as they come up. When you think something negative or catch yourself replaying an old negative memory, stop yourself and use that moment to reprogram your mind. Tell yourself a new truth, a new story, or devise a new way of looking at things. Shift your thoughts about the situation until you feel better. Repeat daily or as often as needed.

Reprogramming yourself as things come up is important because you're able to have in-the-moment awareness and then make a conscious decision to think, feel, believe, and act differently. The more you can do this, the more it will stick.

REFERENCE THIS

If you want to go deeper into the concepts from this chapter, read the following:

In *F*ck the How*:
- Chapter 4: Become A Vibrational Match For What You Want

In *Quantum Leap Your Life*:
- Chapter 2: Believing
- Chapter 4: Thinking

I = INNER WORK
AKA CLEAR OUT AND REPROGRAM

I'm going to share with you an analogy that came to me a few months ago when I was teaching the inaugural round of The Manifest Method course (more about the course at the end of this book). I was trying to find a visual way to explain manifestation. In meditation one morning, I saw this: *Imagine track and field hurdles. You have the end of the track—the finish line—and you have the starting point. In between are these obstacles that you need to jump over to continue moving forward and get to your goal of crossing the finish line.*

Manifestation works similarly. There's the thing you desire to have (the finish line), and there's where you are right now (your starting point). In between there are obstacles, such as limiting beliefs or old inner baggage that you still need to let go of, and negative mindsets that aren't helpful to you having what you want.

When you clear the obstacles, you get to have what you want. And you know there are obstacles because if there weren't, you'd already have it.

Seeing manifestation from this vantage point changed things for me. I stopped making manifesting such a big deal and started to see that it's simply just clearing any obstacles between yourself and the thing you want.

When there are no obstacles, when you know what you want and have no inner stuff going on about it, that's when it shows up fast. This could happen with every manifestation, but your mind has all kinds of thoughts, beliefs, perspectives, judgments, attitudes, etc., about the things you want. Those are often the obstacles that get in the way of you having it. You must change the way you think about it and see what you want from a new vantage point. You simply need to find a way to change your mind about it.

One obstacle a lot of people deal with is the belief that some manifestations are "bigger" than others and require more time and effort. But the actual truth is, there is no "big" or "small" to the Universe. It can bring you the "big" thing you want just as easily as it can a front-row parking space if you believed it was possible and saw it as inevitable.

And that's what it means to do the inner work.

GET YOUR MIND RIGHT

The inner work—as in step four of the Manifest Method—is bringing to the surface and then clearing out, releasing, and/or reprogramming any thoughts, beliefs, mindsets, perspectives, judgments, or feelings that don't align with you having what you want. As one of my favorite authors, Amanda Frances says, *"Anything that says you can't have what you want is a lie."*

Your job is to see what obstacles are there for you with regard to what you want and/or you having what you want, and then start to release and reprogram those things. Do this inner work/mindset reprogramming all day every day until it becomes automatic for you.

Inner work is a continual journey that goes on for the rest of your life. There will always be inner work to do. Sometimes it will be really simple, like just deciding not to believe an old limiting story about yourself anymore. Other times, it will require a deeper dive into why you believe something, where the story came from, choosing a new way to think or believe about it, and then repeating it over and over again until your subconscious mind gets the message. And other times, you may even need to go further and speak with a therapist, coach, or trauma-informed counselor.

The important thing is that you give yourself the permission and the space to heal and release whatever needs to be healed and released. There's no need for you to carry old life baggage with you anymore. You get to decide that today is the day you set it all down and create something new for yourself.

REFERENCE THIS

If you want to go deeper into the concepts from this chapter, read the following:

In *F*ck the How*:
- Chapter 4: Become A Vibrational Match For What You Want

In *Quantum Leap Your Life*:
- Chapter 2: Believing
- Chapter 4: Thinking

F = FEEL IT

AKA BECOME A VIBRATIONAL MATCH TO WHAT YOU WANT

Everything in our world is made of energy, including you and your thoughts, beliefs, feelings, and perspectives. The things you desire to have—tangibly and intangibly—are also made of energy. Because everything is made of energy, it's also vibrating at a molecular level (aka the Law of Vibration). Since everything is vibrating, it all has its own vibrational frequency. That frequency attracts things that have the same or a similar frequency and repels everything else (aka the Law of Attraction).

You have to match the vibrational frequency of what you want in order to receive it. The way you do that is by asking yourself: *What do I believe I will feel once I have that thing?* Get clear on what you believe the specific emotions will be for you when you get what you want. Will you feel excited, proud, and joyful? Or peaceful, aligned, and free? Figure out what the specific emotions would be. That's how you know what the vibrational frequency is of what you want.

If you want a new car, and you believe that having it will

make you feel free and happy, and give you peace of mind, that's the vibrational frequency of that car for you—free, happy, and peaceful. If you want to receive the car, feel free, happy, and peaceful now. When you do, you're matching the vibration of what you want.

And if you don't know or can't figure out what the specific emotions would be, just focus on feeling good in general. Feeling good is the point and the path. Every single thing you desire is because you believe having it will be a positive emotional experience for you. Create a feel-good, positive emotional experience in your life right now, before you have what you want, and it will come to you.

A QUICK LESSON IN FEELING THE FEELS

Once you know what specific emotions (or feeling good, in general) you will feel having what you want, you can look at two things:

- **Where in my life do I already feel those emotions?**
- **What else can I bring into my life that will help me feel those emotions?**

Wherever in your life you already feel those emotions, do more of that. Spend more time with that activity, that person, that place, that thing. As you do so, you're matching the vibration of what you want.

And then look at what else you could start doing or bring into your life that would also create more of those same feelings for you. Implement some of those things in whatever way you can.

REMOVE OR REFRAME EVERYTHING ELSE

There may be people, places, situations, things, etc., going on in your life that don't make you feel very good. They may even make you feel things that are opposite to how you actually want to feel. Allowing those things to remain in your life will cause you to repel what you want because you're not being a vibrational match when you're feeling negative emotions all the time.

This is not to say that you should bypass anything negative and never feel those emotions. Not at all. But you get to choose the emotional states you live in and experience most often. And when things don't make you feel good, you get to look at them and decide if they need to be in your life anymore or not.

You may find that friendship with Little Miss Judgey Judgerson isn't going to cut it anymore. Or that it's time for a new job. Or that you're really just ready to stop calling yourself "stupid" after you make a mistake.

And if the negative—or negative-emotion-producing—thing can't be removed from your life, you can instead look at how to shift it in some way. Either shift the thing itself or how you're doing it or change your perspective on it.

Do whatever you need to do to make the things you can't remove from your life feel good or better than they do right now, just to give yourself some emotional relief.

The more you can feel good and/or feel the specific emotions you desire to feel, the more often you're being a vibrational match to what you want. When you're in that state, you'll be more receptive to the inner nudges, inspired actions, and divine downloads (as I call them) that lead to the How of getting what you want.

Do the inner work, check in on how you're feeling, and shift when needed all day every day.

REFERENCE THIS

If you want to go deeper into the concepts from this chapter, read the following:

In *F*ck the How*:
- Chapter 4: Become A Vibrational Match For What You Want

In *Quantum Leap Your Life*:
- Chapter 3: Feeling

E = EMBODY IT
AKA BECOME THE VERSION OF YOURSELF WHO ALREADY HAS THE THING YOU WANT

When you've embodied something, you've become it. It's who you are. You and it are one.

If someone tells someone else that they're "an inspiration," what they're saying is that person has embodied the qualities and traits of someone who can spark a light in others. But this person wasn't always the embodiment of that. They most likely found themselves living a life they weren't happy with and they decided to change something. In doing so, they became the physical representation of something. In this example, they represent inspiration.

You must do the same and become the version of yourself who already has the thing you want. When you've embodied being that version of yourself—energetically, mentally, and through practical action—you will have what you desire.

To do this, you take on the identity of that version of you through your:

- Thoughts
- Beliefs
- Feelings
- Actions

When you take on the thoughts, beliefs, and feeling states that version of you would be experiencing, you will automatically start to take the actions that match. And the actions won't feel like such a struggle because you'll be feeling more like that version of yourself. Another way of saying this is acting as if.

ACT AS IF THAT'S ALREADY WHO YOU ARE

Sports heroes like Kobe Bryant and Michael Jordan were great behind the scenes when no one was watching long before they were ever great in public. And it's that greatness curated in private that allowed them to become icons. Since they were acting as if they were already icons from the beginning, they also eventually became the physical embodiment of greatness.

The movie, *AIR*, tells a fictional version of the real-life story of how Nike made the life-changing sneaker deal with then-pro-basketball rookie, Michael Jordan. In the beginning, Jordan didn't want anything to do with Nike. Wouldn't even take a meeting with them. He only took one in the end because his mom made him (he was young and had just been drafted to play for the Bulls). But Nike saw something in him that the other brands didn't see. They saw that he was going to be the greatest. One of a kind. A legend. They saw in him what he saw and had been cultivating in himself for his entire life. And that's why he ultimately decided to work with them.

Why am I telling you all of this? Because this is what it takes to manifest the things you want—but most especially the things you consider to be the "bigger" things. You must be that version of yourself first. You must see yourself as that person. And you must take action from a place of being there already, not from still trying to get there.

If Michael Jordan had signed with Converse like everyone pretty much expected him to, he would've been just another basketball player wearing Converse sneakers. But Jordan knew who he was and who he was going to be. He believed in himself and in that version of himself. And he took action from that place. Signing with Nike allowed him to be, not one of several, but the One.

Jordan acted from a place of knowing he was going to be the greatest of all time and chose the brand deal that best aligned with that knowing. And he revolutionized the basketball shoe game forever.

Or at least that's what happened in the movie. And I think you get the point I'm making.

When you know what you want, and who you want to be as that version of yourself, you can start to act as if that's who you are already. The more you do this, the more you'll believe it, and eventually you will actually be the person who has everything you desire and more.

REFERENCE THIS

If you want to go deeper into the concepts from this chapter, read the following:

In *F*ck the How*:
- Chapter 4: Become A Vibrational Match For What You Want

In *Quantum Leap Your Life*:
- Chapter 5: Acting As If

S = SHOW UP FOR YOUR LIFE
AKA STOP WAITING AND LIVE YOUR LIFE RIGHT NOW

How many times have you thought about or said to yourself, "I'll do XYZ thing when [insert the condition you've put between you and having what you want]." So that might look like this:

- *I'll start dating again once I lose 30 pounds.*
- *I'll spend the morning golfing after I retire.*
- *Once I have the house I want, then I'll decorate and make my space feel vibey.*
- *I'll take that pottery class next year when I have more free time.*
- *I'll buy those shoes I want once I get a raise at my job.*

The problem with all of those statements and others like them is you're using them as an excuse to put your life on hold. It's placing conditions on you being able to have, do, or be what you want. And that's not how manifesting works.

Manifesting is not about the actual thing you want. It's not about the house or the car or the relationship or the happiness or whatever you desire to have. It's about the journey of co-creating it with the Universe.

Once you manifest the thing you want, it's going to feel so natural that it will almost be anticlimactic. You may not even enjoy it as much as you thought, and there will likely already be something else you want. Dreams and desires never die. And there's nothing wrong with that. Dreams and desires are tools to help you get clear on what you want and what your life is meant to be about. They're a path to follow to a life beyond your wildest imagination.

But the point is the path getting there, not the dream or desire itself. Get it?

So this is why it's pointless to put anything off, especially if it's something you really want to be doing, being, or having. Maybe you can't do it in full right now. But there's some aspect of it you can probably start doing. And that will help you create the belief and feelings you need to bring about the full manifestation.

You have to—even when things aren't how you want them to be yet—find a way to enjoy something anyhow. You may not be able to feel positive emotions about everything going on in your life, but there should be at least one thing that makes you feel something positive. Doesn't matter what it is. The good feelings—even in small doses—are more powerful than the negative ones.

Every day, every week, month, and year, just do what you would be doing if you knew what you wanted was a done deal and you weren't worried about it. Live your life. Do what you enjoy. Stop putting things off.

DO WHAT YOU KNOW TO DO ACTIONS

In the previous chapter, we talked about embodiment actions, which is when you act as if you're already the version of yourself who has what you want. The other kind of action is what I call Do What You Know To Do actions.

These are the actions that logically make sense for you to be doing with regard to the thing you want and are manifesting. If, for example, you want to be a successful artist, a do-what-you-know-to-do action would be to sit down and make art or take a class and learn more or interview another artist to see what it's like to be one.

When you act as if and take do what you know to do actions as a way of living fully and showing up for your life, you're not only being a vibrational match to what you want, but you're putting yourself into a receptive energy so the Universe can reach you with its nudges, ideas, downloads, hows, etc.

Act as if, do what you know to do, and show up for your life while you manifest the things you want.

REFERENCE THIS

If you want to go deeper into the concepts from this chapter, read the following:

In *F*ck the How*:
Chapter 5: Live Your Damn Life

Bonus Reference:
My book, *Test Drive Your Dreams*

T = TAKE INSPIRED ACTION
AKA WHEN YOU FEEL INSPIRED TO TAKE AN ACTION, TRUST YOURSELF AND DO IT

You can probably think of a time when you were just sitting around or doing some kind of mindless activity and then *BAM!* Seemingly out of nowhere, an idea hits your brain. And now you have an action to take, or a solution to something you've needed one for, or something new to create. Or maybe you've felt this inner nudge or pull to do something for a while now, but you just haven't acted on it yet.

What you have just experienced is inspired action. You received inspiration from the Universe to do something or say something or go somewhere, whatever it might be for you.

Now you have to do something with it.

What most people do is sit around questioning themselves or worrying about whether they should do it or not. This is a waste of time and only creates split energy. My personal rule is, when I get a divine download (aka inspired action) for something that feels really good to me, I move on it, regardless of how scary, challenging, or intimidating it might be. I act on my divine downloads, period. No matter what. Now I get more inspired actions, ideas, nudges, downloads, etc., than I could ever use or do anything with.

CHOOSE THE INSPIRATION THAT FEELS GOOD

Make it non-negotiable that you only choose the inspired ideas, actions, etc., that feel good to you. Yes, the idea or action might feel a little challenging, confronting, or intimidating, but when you think about being on the other side of it, you know you'll be glad you did it. That's how you know which inspired actions are the right ones for you.

Let all other forced actions or ideas go for the time being.

READY YOURSELF TO RECEIVE INSPO

There are a couple of things you can do to make yourself more open and available to receive inspiration:

- **Clear your mind clutter daily**—Our minds are so cluttered and full of stuff, but if you don't find a way to quiet some of that noise, you won't be able to hear the inspired ideas and actions as easily. My two favorite ways to clear mind clutter are freestyle stream-of-consciousness journaling and meditation.
- **Pay attention more often**—The more you can keep yourself present in the moment, the more you'll be able to see and/or hear the divine guidance, inspiration, and nudges.

NO MATTER WHAT, FIND A WAY TO TRUST

Let's look at the definition of trust for a second. *Oxford Languages* defines trust as: "A firm belief in the reliability, truth, ability or strength of someone or something." This is the definition I like the best because it gives you a very clear understanding of what trust is.

Trust is a firm belief in the reliability and truth of something. And how do you create a firm belief in something's reliability or truth? You test it out. You start with something "small" that you don't have resistance to and go from there.

Trust isn't always the easiest thing for humans. We've been programmed with so many limiting societal, cultural, religious, and familial beliefs that it can be hard to trust in anything, let alone something you can't see with your physical senses.

But that's another part of your inner work. To learn how to trust that something bigger and greater than yourself is always co-creating with you and wants to help you make all of your dreams and desires a reality.

And then you have to keep going until what you want or something even better shows up. Those who do, eventually get what they want, and those who don't... well, don't.

REFERENCE THIS

If you want to go deeper into the concepts from this chapter, read the following:

In *F*ck the How*:
- Chapter 6: Take Inspired Action
- Chapter 7: Trust and Keep Going

In *Quantum Leap Your Life*:
- Chapter 6: It Takes As Long As It Takes

A MANIFEST METHOD EXAMPLE
AKA HOW I USED THE MANIFEST METHOD TO MANIFEST LOVE

M = MASSIVE CLARITY

Months after I manifested my divorce, I was coming around to the idea of meeting someone new. After all, I still didn't have what I'd asked the Universe for the year prior. While I did manifest a divorce from the relationship that was no longer right for me, that was only the halfway point. What I wanted was the love and relationship I desired. So there was still more journey to go on.

But the idea of spending hours of my time swiping left and right on dating apps, and having convos or dates with random guys in hopes of finding someone good just felt like a whole lot of unnecessary effort. I didn't want to date. I just wanted to find my person. So I decided to use the Manifest Method and manifest him instead.

I knew what I didn't want, having had my previous marriage and relationships to use as contrast. That helped me get clear on what I did want, including things I wouldn't have given myself permission to want previously, like for him to be an entrepreneur and have his money shit together.

I pulled a spiral notebook out from a pile of notebooks that I randomly used and opened it to a fresh page. At the top, I wrote: *What I want in a man and relationship*. Below it, I listed out all of the characteristics and attributes I wanted the man to have, in general, along with a few non-negotiable specifics. I went deep and even wrote down stuff like what I wanted his mindset to be like and what kind of person I wanted him to be.

I painted as clear of a picture with my words as I could for the Universe, while still leaving room to be pleasantly surprised.

A = ADVANCED GRATITUDE

After I made my list of everything I wanted in a man and relationship, in general, and specifically, I said a surrender statement out loud to the Universe. I don't do it this way anymore, but this was back before I knew what I now know. At the time, the only way I could truly let something go and delegate it to the Universe was if I said a surrender statement (now I would just thank the Universe in advance for making it happen).

So I said my statement: "*Universe, what I've written on this list is what I want. This or something better. It's what I deserve and know I'm worthy of. I don't know how to find this person, so I'm delegating it to you to find him for me. I will do my part and take action on any nudges you send me. I trust that you will find the perfect person for me. Thank you.*" Or something like that. I don't remember the exact words, but you get the vibe of my intention.

I knew what I wanted. I decided on it. I was grateful for it ahead of time. After I said my surrender statement, I closed the notebook and put it away.

And then I went about living my life.

N = NOW DECIDE YOU'RE WORTHY

Without realizing it, I had somehow taken on a "between relationships" guy. He was a guy friend I'd known for nearly twenty years, and any time during those years we were both single, we'd hook up. We never officially dated, we were just friends with benefits. And so it was no surprise to me that this pattern repeated after my divorce.

As usual, I walked away from the experience feeling how I always did—momentary elation, followed by a tidal wave of self-doubt and disappointment. The truth is, I never felt good enough for this guy. I never felt like I measured up to his standards. Never felt like I could be who or what he wanted. And I used to let that make me doubt my worthiness.

I'm not blaming him. It wasn't at all his fault. Those were just the feelings he triggered inside of me. But rather than asking why he triggered those feelings, I instead asked myself something I never had before: *Why am I continuing to put myself into situations with this guy where I come out feeling unworthy and not good enough?*

I decided I was done involving myself in that way with this guy. I was done allowing myself to feel that way anymore. There was really no reason for me to pursue the situation any further. He had shown me for nearly two decades that he was just not that into me, and I decided to finally believe him.

I decided I was worthy, deserving, and good enough to

have the kind of guy and relationship I wanted. I put my stake in the ground and chose to believe in my worth.

It was a huge leap for me in the direction of reclaiming my worthiness in dating and relationships.

And I'm not one to bypass how I feel or let myself off the hook when I notice something internally that needs deeper introspection. So I also made a list of the specific things—like my worthiness, how I saw myself, and beliefs around what I got to have—that I needed to do some massive reprogramming around.

I = INNER WORK

After my divorce, I moved back to my hometown to be closer to my family. I wanted to see my nephew grow up and not be an absentee aunt. But I had a problem because I've always had a love-hate relationship with the place I grew up. I never really liked living there and always thought it was such a backward behind-the-times place. I also had never dated there as an adult because I moved away when I left for college at age seventeen.

And one of the biggest limiting beliefs I had going on was that the kind of guy I was looking for wouldn't live where I lived. I believed a guy who would match the qualities and interests I was looking for would have to live somewhere more new-age-y, like California or Portland, Oregon. Except I didn't want to live in those places. I wanted to live where my nephew lives.

So I had to do the work to release and reprogram that—and many other—limiting beliefs.

Every morning, I sat down to do my daily mindset practice,

and I made sure to include new beliefs about finding my dream guy right where I lived, and that no matter where I chose to live, everything I desired would still always be mine and available for me.

Funnily enough, the Universe soon sent me evidence of this being true, and I was able to believe even more.

I received a text message from one of my girlfriends from college, letting me know that my college crush was not only single again, but actively looking for love (she found his profile on a dating app she was on). Since she knew I was single again, she figured I would want to know this information.

I ended up sending him a message on Facebook Messenger and we started chatting about life. Soon, the conversation turned to manifesting and how he had become much more spiritual over the last year. It was like sirens went off in my head—*Hello! A guy who matches the kind of guy you want is literally sitting here talking to you about all the things you've always dreamed of AND he lives near where you live. The Universe orchestrated this to show you that you can have whatever you want so long as you choose to believe it!*

That solidified a whole new way of seeing myself and what was possible for me. And while my college crush wasn't the guy for me in real life, he was a perfect bit of evidence that helped me to believe I would one day find that guy.

F = FEEL IT

There's a feel-good playlist of songs on my phone that I've curated over the years. Each song makes me feel something good. Whether it's the lyrics or just the music, each song moves my energy to a higher-vibe state. And on that playlist are several songs that help me to deeply feel the emotion of love.

When I listen to those specific songs, I feel my dream relationship. When I hear that music, those lyrics, I know true love is real and it exists and it's available for me. I can't explain why it does that, other than it's just a feeling I get.

So during the time I was manifesting the love and relationship I desired to have, I was listening to those songs daily, on repeat. I was also watching and rewatching my favorite romantic movies and love scenes from my favorite TV shows.

Most importantly, I was feeling the emotion of love inside of myself as much as possible. I truly felt like I already had the love and relationship I desired to have, even if I didn't physically have it just yet.

E = EMBODY IT

A big part of me embodying the love and relationship I desired to have was when I decided to stop involving myself with guys who made me feel unworthy or not good enough. That was a huge leap for me. But there was more to it than that.

I realized that I had to start giving myself whatever I wanted to receive from someone else. I had to create a better, more accepting, and loving relationship with myself first if I was ever going to have that with another person.

I started looking for ways I could love myself more. Anything from a consistent fitness habit to cutting down on sugar to spending an hour wandering the stacks at the public library and taking home a dozen new books to read. I took myself on "dates." I found a new local restaurant I loved and frequented it. I bought myself flowers from the grocery store. I did the things I wanted to be doing and experiencing with someone else.

I acted as if I already had the love and relationship I wanted. Because I did have it, with myself. And once I had it with myself, I was a vibrational match to having it in my physical life as well.

S = SHOW UP FOR YOUR LIFE

One weekend not too long after I made my list and started doing the inner and outer work to become a vibrational match to what I wanted, it was my cousin's birthday. We were all at my aunt's house for cake and presents. Then when everyone was getting ready to leave, my cousin's boyfriend at the time said, *"Why don't we go out for a birthday drink?"*

So we all went out to this local bar and grill to have a drink. When we sat down at our table, I noticed this guy at the table across from us staring at me. When I looked over at him, he smiled. I smiled back. And thus began an evening of smiling back and forth until finally toward the end of the night, the guy signaled for me to meet him over at the bar.

I went over to talk to him for a few minutes. We had so much in common right off the bat and we talked for a while. After, we exchanged numbers and he left. As I was walking back to the table where my family was, I saw a shiny penny looking up at me from the ground. And when I went to save his number in my phone, I saw that it had seven-seven-seven in it. (In case you don't know yet, seven-seven-seven and coins on the ground are two of the signs I typically receive from the Universe.)

It felt like the Universe had orchestrated all of this. So

when he texted to invite me to brunch the next day, I decided to go and see what happened. We had a great time and ended up talking for more than three hours about every topic under the sun, including manifesting and mindset. I never thought I'd find a guy who lived in my city and wanted to talk about these kinds of things, and yet here we were. Not only that, but he was the one bringing up a lot of the topics.

And while this guy wasn't the right one for me (we had decided to just be friends), he became a shining example from the Universe that the kind of guy I wanted lived where I live. This guy was the evidence I received after doing all of that inner/mindset and belief work. The Universe was showing me what I wanted was not only possible and available, but available at home.

My limiting belief was demolished and I became an even better vibrational match to receiving the love and relationship I desired to have.

T = TAKE INSPIRED ACTION

Since that guy and I were friends, we decided to meet up for a drink one Thursday night after he got off work. I work for myself, so I was home all day doing my thing, and then later on I got ready to go out. Unfortunately, he ended up texting me to say he was stuck at work and had to reschedule.

Usually, I would stay home and watch a movie or something, but that night, I just really wanted a glass of wine. I thought about buying a bottle so I could have a drink at home, but I knew most of the bottle would end up going to waste, and I was already dressed up. I wanted to go out.

So I went out anyhow. Alone. I went to Bar Louie where we

were supposed to meet for a drink, and I sat at the bar and had a drink all by myself. I mean, I wasn't alone-alone. There were people everywhere. It was Thirsty Thursday, after all.

I was feeling pretty good sitting there. I felt proud for not canceling plans on myself just because someone else couldn't go with me. It felt like I was starting to become the version of me I wanted to be. Someone who showed up for herself and her desires, and didn't let anyone or anything get in the way.

While I sat there, drinking my glass of Moscato, I decided to check my emails. I was scrolling through my inbox when I came across an email from a dating app I had an account with.

The year prior, when I was still married, I wrote a screenplay about dating apps, but I had never been on a dating app before so I didn't know what they were actually like. After my divorce, I decided to sign up for a few of them to see what they were like and check the accuracy of my screenplay.

But since this was a paid app, I never actually signed up or paid, I just set the account up. I felt an inner nudge to open the email so I did. I don't know why, but I trusted it. The email said I had thirty-five unread messages and it offered me a discount to try the dating app for a month. I had never tried anything like that before, so I decided to give it a try for thirty days. What could it hurt?

Once I was signed up, I logged in and discovered that I did have thirty-five messages. I deleted all but one of the messages. The one I saved was from this guy named Dave. He had very little info or pics on his dating profile, and his message only had a few words in it, but I was magnetized.

I replied back to him. He replied back to me, and we ended up texting inside the app for a few hours. We exchanged numbers, started texting each other nonstop, and five days later we met in person. The rest, as they say, is history.

And because the Universe has a sense of humor and loves to show off, he not only lived in my city and my town, but his house was less than two miles away from mine, and his street was off of another street called Weiland Rd. (Weiland is the name of my dog.) You can't make this shit up.

Not only that, but he ended up matching every single general thing I wrote on my list, and almost all of the specifics. The only specific he didn't match was that I wrote down I wanted a guy who didn't have a pet. Not that I have anything against pets, but my dog isn't great with other dogs. He doesn't like them and doesn't want to be around them (he's a prissy toy poodle like that). My boyfriend also had a dog. I knew this from the get-go and yet for some reason, it didn't deter me. I was a little worried, yes, but I was also very curious.

I had clearly manifested him, he was an insanely good match for me, and he had a dog. There had to be a reason the Universe brought us together. It felt how I wanted it to feel, so I decided to trust what showed up.

As it turns out, his dog is the only dog on the planet my dog gets along with. So now my dog gets to have a dog brother. That is something I never would've known or thought to ask for, but the Universe always sees more and knows better. It sent me the perfect guy for me with the perfect dog for my dog.

That's the power of the Manifest Method. And that's why I now use it to manifest everything, no matter what it is, without ever worrying about how I'll do it.

THE MANIFEST METHOD CHEATSHEET

This entire book is meant to be one big cheatsheet for manifesting your version of the dream life. But I also wanted you to have a one-page overview that could act as a quick reference for the methodology when you want or need a reminder.

The cheatsheet lists out each step in the Manifest Method, along with the most important things to remember or consider within each step.

To view this one-page cheatsheet, turn to the next page. And to get a PDF copy you can download, print out, and post in your living space, go here:

www.jenniferblanchard.net/cheatsheet

The Manifest Method CHEATSHEET

M — Massive clarity

Decide what you want, either specifically or in general

- Be as specific as you can get behind/believe in
- Go general to decrease resistance
- Use triggers, resentment, jealousy and contrast to give you further clarity

A — Advance gratitude

Be grateful in advance of having what you want, as if you already have it

- Thank the Universe in advance
- Surrender it, let it go, release it
- Return to the Four Truths of Surrender
- Know it's always this (what you want) or something better you don't know about yet

N — Now decide you're worthy

Decide you are worthy, good enough and deserving

- Decide your worth is no longer a question or in question
- Release and reprogram any thoughts, beliefs, or old memories that don't match
- Repeat daily or as needed

I — Inner work

Clear out and reprogram

- Release and reprogram any thoughts, beliefs, feelings, mindsets, perspectives, or judgments that don't align with you having what you want
- Do this work all day every day until it becomes automatic for you

F — Feel it

Become a vibrational match to what you want

- Figure out the specific emotions you'd feel having it and feel it now
- What already makes you feel that way? Do more of that.
- Or just feel good in general
- Remove or reframe anything that doesn't feel good to you
- Do this work daily

E — Embody it

Become the version of yourself who already has the thing you want

- Take on the identity--thoughts, beliefs, feelings and actions--of you having what you want
- Act as if that's already who you are
- See yourself as that version of you
- Take action from a place of being there already not having to get there still

S — Show up for your life

Live your life right now

- Stop waiting, stop putting life off "until"
- Enjoy the day to day journey
- Do what you would be doing if you knew what you want is a done deal and you weren't worried about it
- Live your dream life however you can from where you are right now

T — Take inspired action

When you feel inspired to take an action, trust yourself and do it

- Act on any inner-nudges, or inspired ideas or actions that feel good to you
- Clear your mind clutter, pay attention more
- Trust the Universe and keep going until you get what you want or something even better

To download a PDF version of this cheatsheet, go to: www.jenniferblanchard.net/cheatsheet

The Manifest Method Cheatsheet | Copyright 2023 Jennifer Blanchard | All Rights Reserved

PART TWO
THE WORKBOOK

You get to have your version of having "it all." Whatever "it all" means to you. And your version may not look like anyone else's. That's the point. You want things for yourself and your life that not everyone else does. You're unique and special, and you get to have everything you want and more. But first, you need to get clear on what having "it all" means for you. Once you know what you want, you can use the Manifest Method to create it.

I'm a workbook person. I love having a place I can go back to over and over again to work through a process. For example, I have a workbook that I use when I'm writing my novels—it walks me step by step through my process for planning out a story—so I cover the foundation. I find processes and methods and workbooks helpful. Maybe it's just me. If it is, you can totally ignore the rest of this book and go on using the Manifest Method in your life in whatever way works best for you. (I also recommend checking out the additional resources at the end of this book.)

But if you're like me, and you prefer to write things down and really dig into a process, especially when you're first learning how to embody it, this is the tool for you. Part Two of this book is a workbook you can use to work through the Manifest Method with one or more of the things you want to manifest.

There's no wrong way to use this workbook. Write in the actual book, copy the questions and/or responses over to a journal, or type it out on your computer, whatever you prefer.

You can grab a PDF copy of the workbook here: www.jenniferblanchard.net/meworkbook

For best results, I recommend starting with "M" and then going through the remainder of the process. I also recommend doing it separately, at least at first, for each thing you want to manifest, as you will likely have different limiting beliefs, stories, mindsets, actions, etc., come up for each one.

Once you've done this a handful of times and get used to the process, it will become a lot more natural and you'll find yourself doing the steps automatically and without needing to go through the effort of writing it all down. I do a lot of this process in my head these days, though I always love those moments when I pull out my workbook or journal and write things down.

If you have questions after you go through the workbook or want to share any insights or results that show up, you can drop by my free Facebook group, The Feel-Good Life Club: www.facebook.com/groups/feelgoodlifecenter.

MANIFEST ANYTHING

Recommendation: *Choose one thing you want to manifest and work through this workbook with that one thing. Once you've done this a few times, you'll get better at using the process.*

M: MASSIVE CLARITY

Your goal in this section of the workbook is to decide what you want, either specifically or in general.

As a reminder:

- Only be specific about the things you can get behind and/or fully believe in
- Be more general to decrease any resistance you feel, or
- Increase your belief level so it matches the specific thing you want, or
- Focus only on the specifics that are non-negotiable, and be general with the rest

So... **What do you want?**

_____

_____

_____

Another way of asking it: **What do you desire? What do you dream of?**

_____

_____

_____

_____

_____

What is the vision you see for yourself and your life (or any specific area of your life)? Write it out. And if you don't have a vision yet, use this space to play around and imagine what your life would be like if you could have anything.

_____

_____

_____

_____

_____

_____

_____

_____

Now let's get even more clarity:

Are you experiencing contrast in any area(s) of your life right now? What do you want in that area instead?

_____
_____
_____
_____
_____
_____

Is there anything going on or anyone in your life who triggers you? Why does it bother you? What dream or desire could be hidden inside of it?

_____
_____
_____
_____
_____
_____
_____
_____
_____

Where in your life do you feel resentful, jealous, or angry that someone else has what you want? Have you given yourself full permission to have it yet? Be totally honest with yourself. There's no judgment on this page.

_____
_____

_____
_____
_____
_____
_____
_____

What would you want if you weren't worried about the money or how you'll pay for it?

_____
_____
_____
_____
_____
_____

What would you want if you weren't worried about the how of getting it, being it, doing it, or having it? If the how didn't matter, what would you want?

_____
_____
_____
_____
_____
_____

. . .

If guilt, shame, and judgment were no longer a thing, what would you want?

_____
_____
_____
_____
_____
_____
_____
_____

What did you want as a kid that still calls to you today?

_____
_____
_____
_____
_____
_____
_____
_____

If you wouldn't lose anyone and no one would get mad at you, what would you want?

_____
_____

_____
_____
_____
_____
_____
_____

After going through these questions for deeper clarity, ask yourself again: **What do I want?**

_____
_____
_____
_____
_____
_____

What do you want in the next thirty days? Ninety days? Six months? One year?

_____
_____
_____
_____
_____

_____
_____

Intend that you will have it—this or something better—and then DECIDE! Give yourself permission to want what you actually want.

A: ADVANCE GRATITUDE

Your goal in this section of the workbook is to be grateful in advance of having what you want, as if you already have it.

Now that you know what you want, say thank you for it in advance. *Thank you Universe for [insert what you're being grateful in advance for].* Your turn...

Thank you Universe/God/Source for:

_____
_____
_____
_____
_____
_____
_____

Repeat this phrase after your thank you statement: **And so it is.**

. . .

Think about the things you already have in your life right now that you're grateful for, and take a minute to express that gratitude in the space below. The key is to only write down the things you can truly feel the emotion of gratitude for (as opposed to things you think you should be grateful for).

_____
_____
_____
_____
_____
_____
_____

Any time you catch yourself worrying about it, or having a hard time trusting, again say thank you in advance for it. Repeat as often as needed.

And whenever necessary, return to **the Four Truths of Surrender:**

- The Universe is on it the moment you have gratitude in advance for it.
- It's working even when you can't see it with your physical senses yet (especially when you can't).
- It's working better than you can ever imagine.
- For every one step you take, the Universe takes more.

This is all you need to do to start applying the gratitude in advance concept in your life. The more you practice, the better you'll get at being able to say your advance gratitude statement and then let it go and trust that the Universe will deliver.

But let's keep going.

What else can you now hand over, delegate, or surrender to the Universe? Make a list:

_____
_____
_____
_____
_____
_____
_____
_____

What's the most challenging thing for you when it comes to surrendering, and how can you shift this?

_____
_____
_____
_____
_____
_____
_____
_____

. . .

And for those times when you know what you want, but are doubting it or worrying about it, here's a surrender statement you can use to help pull you out of it (adapted from the one in my book, *F*ck the How*):

Dear Universe/God/Source,

I want to feel good and I can no longer put energy into worrying or trying to figure out what to do about/how to get [insert what you want]. So I'm handing it over and delegating it to you to figure it out for me.

Thank you for [insert what you want the Universe to do/figure out for you, either specifically or in general]. I trust that you've got this and will handle it for me. I'm willing to stay out of the way while you work your magic. I will do my part and act on any inspired actions, ideas, or nudges that you send me.

And so it is.

Fill out this blank statement or write yours out below:

Dear Universe/God/Source,

I want to feel good and I can no longer put energy into worrying or trying to figure out what to do about/how to get _____. So I'm handing it over and delegating it to you to figure it out for me. Thank you for _____.

I trust that you've got this and will handle it for me. I'm willing to stay out of the way while you work your magic. I will do my part and act on any inspired actions, ideas, or nudges that you send me.

And so it is.

_____
_____
_____
_____
_____
_____

N: NOW DECIDE YOU'RE WORTHY

Your goal in this section of the workbook is to decide you are worthy, good enough, and deserving to have what you want, now and forevermore.

Do you feel worthy, deserving and good enough to have the thing you want and had advance gratitude for?

_____
_____

Why or why not?

_____
_____

_____
_____
_____
_____
_____
_____

If you said you don't yet feel worthy, here are more questions to dive into:

What in your life experience has told you, taught you, or made you believe that you're not good enough/worthy?

_____
_____
_____
_____
_____
_____
_____

What have been the consequences of believing this about yourself for so long? How has it affected your life?

_____
_____
_____

_____
_____
_____
_____
_____
_____

What would you do, be, have, and/or go for in your life if you felt worthy and good enough?

_____
_____
_____
_____
_____
_____
_____

What conditions have you placed on you being worthy, good enough, and deserving?

_____
_____
_____
_____
_____
_____
_____

. . .

What would happen if you chose to remove those conditions?

_____
_____
_____
_____
_____
_____
_____

What becomes possible for you when you no longer doubt your worthiness?

_____
_____
_____
_____
_____
_____
_____

If your worth was no longer a question or in question, then what?

_____
_____
_____

MANIFEST EVERYTHING

_____
_____
_____
_____
_____

What can you now choose to believe instead about you being worthy, deserving, and good enough?

_____
_____
_____
_____
_____
_____
_____
_____

What will you do to begin to reclaim your worthiness right now?

_____
_____
_____
_____
_____
_____
_____

_____

Make the decision that from here on out, you are worthy, good enough, and deserving of everything you want to be, do, and have. Write out your decision statement:

_____
_____
_____
_____
_____
_____
_____

I: INNER WORK

Your goal in this section of the workbook is to clear out and reprogram your inner world (subconscious programs, mindset, beliefs, perspective, etc), especially in regard to the thing(s) you're manifesting.

When you think about having what you want—the thing you had advance gratitude for—what beliefs, thoughts, mindsets, perspectives, or judgments come up that tell you that you can't have it?

_____
_____
_____

_____
_____
_____
_____
_____
_____

Are any of the things you just wrote down the only truths that exist? What else could choose to believe instead?

_____
_____
_____
_____
_____
_____
_____
_____

What old memories or limiting stories from your life come up when you think about having what you want?

_____
_____
_____
_____
_____
_____
_____

_____

What have you been making it mean that you don't yet have the thing that you want? And how can you now change the meaning or give it no meaning at all?

_____
_____
_____
_____
_____
_____
_____

What patterns (repetitive unconscious actions or unintended results) do you notice playing out over and over again in any area(s) of your life?

_____
_____
_____
_____
_____
_____
_____

. . .

Who or what taught you that you don't get to have "it all?"

_____
_____
_____
_____
_____
_____
_____

When you think about having your version of "it all," what comes up for you? What fears, doubts, worries, limiting beliefs, old memories, or stories tell you it isn't possible?

_____
_____
_____
_____
_____
_____
_____

Are any of those things you just wrote down in the question above the only truths that exist? What else could choose to believe instead?

_____
_____

_____
_____
_____
_____
_____
_____

Claim what you now choose to believe about yourself, your life, the thing you're manifesting, having "it all," or whatever else you need to claim:

_____
_____
_____
_____
_____
_____
_____
_____

From here on out, whenever you catch yourself thinking or believing something limiting or that doesn't align with you having what you want, here's what to do:

- Stop what you're doing
- Check in on what you were just thinking/believing/feeling

- Ask yourself if this is the only available option for you to be thinking/believing/feeling
- Choose to think, believe and/or feel something else instead
- Think or say positive things until you feel better
- Repeat as needed

F: FEEL IT

Your goal in this section of the workbook is to become a vibrational match to what you want.

What specific emotions do you believe you'll feel when you have the thing you're manifesting? If you're not sure, take a guess:

_____
_____
_____
_____
_____
_____
_____
_____
_____
_____

Where in your life do you already feel those emotions? What in your life makes you feel that way already? List everything out:

_____

_____
_____
_____
_____
_____
_____
_____

What else could you implement, bring in, or start doing in your life right now that would also make you feel those emotions? Brainstorm some ideas:

_____
_____
_____
_____
_____
_____
_____

What makes you feel good, in general? Consider people, places, activities, etc. List out everything you can think of (it's okay if you repeat things from the lists above):

_____
_____
_____

_____
_____
_____
_____

Your responses from the previous three questions are all of the ways that you can become more of a vibrational match to the thing you're manifesting. The positive emotions you're feeling most often matter more than anything else.

But there's more, so let's keep going.

What stops you from feeling good in your life right now?
_____
_____
_____
_____
_____
_____
_____

What people, things, situations, etc., do you have going on in your life right now that don't meet your standards and why?
_____
_____

_____
_____
_____
_____
_____
_____

What needs to change in any area(s) of your life so that you can feel good?

_____
_____
_____
_____
_____
_____
_____
_____

Your responses from the previous three questions are all of the things that you can remove from your life, shift in some way, or reframe your perspective on so that you can feel better.

Tuning into how you're feeling on a daily basis and shifting when you need to is key to becoming and staying a vibrational match to the thing(s) you're manifesting.

E: EMBODY IT

Your goal in this section of the workbook is to become the version of yourself who already has the thing you want (aka embody being the vibrational match for good).

What is the identity of the version of you who has what you want already?

_____
_____
_____
_____
_____
_____
_____

How must you begin to see yourself in order to have and experience more of what you want in your life?

_____
_____
_____
_____
_____
_____
_____

. . .

What would the thoughts, beliefs, and feelings of that version of you be?

_____
_____
_____
_____
_____
_____
_____
_____

What habits would be in place if you were already that version of you?

_____
_____
_____
_____
_____
_____
_____
_____

What would your standards be? What boundaries would you have in place in your life, career, and/or business?

_____

_____
_____
_____
_____
_____
_____
_____

What would you look like as that version of you? How would you dress?

_____
_____
_____
_____
_____
_____
_____

How would you walk? Talk? Eat? Carry yourself? Treat other people? All as the version of you who has what you want.

_____
_____
_____
_____
_____
_____
_____

What would your energy be like? How would you show up in the world?

What would you do differently as the version of yourself who already has what you want?

. . .

How can you begin to act as if you're already that version of yourself by committing to doing some of what you listed out above right now?

_____
_____
_____
_____
_____
_____
_____

When you start to think, believe, feel, act, do, decide, etc., like the version of yourself who already has what you want—even if it hasn't shown up just yet—you are embodying being that person right now, and you're being a vibrational match to what you want.

S: SHOW UP FOR YOUR LIFE

Your goal in this section of the workbook is to find ways to live your dream life right now—no more waiting!

Where in your life are you currently waiting or putting off something you want to be doing?

_____
_____
_____

JENNIFER BLANCHARD

_____
_____
_____
_____

Why are you doing this?

_____
_____
_____
_____
_____
_____

How can you start doing some of what you've been waiting on or putting off right now? In what ways—even small ones—can you take action now?

_____
_____
_____
_____
_____
_____

_____

What can you do to enjoy your life more and live in the moment more often?

_____
_____
_____
_____
_____
_____
_____

How can you have some fun this week/weekend?

_____
_____
_____
_____
_____
_____
_____

What lights you up/excites you? What are you passionate about?

_____

_____

_____

_____

_____

_____

_____

_____

How can you do more of those things you're passionate about and that excite you on a regular basis (daily if possible)?

_____

_____

_____

_____

_____

_____

_____

What else would you be doing in your life right now if you knew that the thing you're manifesting was a done deal and you weren't worried about it?

_____

_____

_____

_____

_____

_____

_____

Live your dream life however you can from the starting point you're at right now—that's what it means to show up for your life. And everything you wrote down in this section will help you to do that.

T: TRUST THE NUDGES

Your goal in this section of the workbook is to trust yourself and take inspired action when you get an idea or feel an inner nudge to.

Before you begin this section, I recommend clearing your mind clutter first. My favorite way to do that is freestyle stream-of-consciousness journaling for at least one full page. You could also meditate, go for a walk, or whatever helps you clear your mind.

What ideas do you currently have for inspired actions you could take? Write them down below:

_____

_____

_____

_____

_____

_____

_____

If you don't have any inspired actions right now, what are some do-what-you-know-to-do actions you could take in the meantime?

_____

_____

_____

_____

_____

_____

ADDITIONAL NOTES

_____

_____

_____

_____

_____

_____

MANIFEST EVERYTHING

_____
_____
_____
_____
_____
_____
_____
_____
_____

THE MANIFESTING TRIFECTA:
MANIFEST EVERYTHING + F*CK THE HOW + QUANTUM LEAP YOUR LIFE

You have this book... and now it's time to also add *F*ck the How*, and *Quantum Leap Your Life* to your library. Those books work together with *Manifest Everything* to give you an even deeper understanding of the spiritual and energetic concepts that will help you manifest more intentionally.

I consider *Manifest Everything* to be a short-and-sweet manifesting cheatsheet, which is awesome if that's what you're looking for.

But if you want to deepen your understanding, see more examples, and embody the elements of this process even further, then *F*ck the How*, and *Quantum Leap Your Life* will round out your Manifesting Trifecta.

And here's a sneak peek at both of those books:

F*CK THE HOW

WHAT IF NOT KNOWING HOW WAS NO LONGER AN OBSTACLE TO YOUR DREAMS AND DESIRES?

THE MANIFESTING TRIFECTA:

The number one reason you're not going for your deepest dreams and desires in life—or even giving yourself full permission to want those things—is because you don't know How you'll make them a reality. Not knowing How then becomes a barrier that stops you from doing, being, or having the things and the life you know you're meant for.

But the truth is, you never, ever, ever, ever need to know How you'll do, be, or have something before you decide that you're going to. No matter what it is you desire and dream of. Even if it's a so-called "pipe dream."

You don't need to know all of the steps. You don't need a strategy or an action plan. You don't have to make a to-do list and check everything off. You don't even have to do most of what you think it takes to do, be, and have what you want.

You just have to do your part and stay the hell out of the way so the Universe can do its part.

*F*ck the How* demystifies manifestation and teaches you the process to go from dream or desire in your heart to actually receiving it in your real, physical life, without ever having to know How beforehand.

Whether you're a creative with big dreams, an overthinker, a control freak, or someone who just gets way too caught up on the How of making your desires happen, this paradigm-shifting book will help you to set the How aside and get any-freaking-thing that you want.

QUANTUM LEAP YOUR LIFE

MANIFEST YOUR DREAM LIFE FASTER THAN EVER BEFORE

If you've ever read a book (or twenty) about manifestation, you've heard that you need to "act as if." But most books don't explain how to do this well enough for you to actually use it in your own life.

This is not one of those books.

In *Quantum Leap Your Life*, author Jennifer Blanchard shows you exactly how to act as if you already have the things that you want—in belief, feeling, thought, and action—before you actually do. She also includes lots of clear examples to help illustrate the principle of acting as if.

It's time for you to make a quantum leap in your life, and close the gap between where you are right now and where you want to be.

Both *F*ck the How*, and *Quantum Leap Your Life* are available on Amazon in eBook and paperback (and hardcover for *F*ck the How*), and also on Audible

—> **Go to: www.dreamlifeorbust.com to complete your Manifesting Trifecta today!**

THE MANIFEST EVERYTHING CRASH COURSE

WANT TO MANIFEST YOUR DREAM LIFE EASIER AND FASTER?

You've come to the right place.

Whether you want to manifest:

- More success in your business
- New love
- A better job
- A vibey apartment
- Time freedom to spend on your creative projects
- Abundance
- A divorce/breakup
- Or ANYTHING in between

This crash course is for you!

Introducing... **the MANIFEST Everything Crash Course!**

I created this Crash Course as a short yet powerful intro to using the MANIFEST Method process.

The 8 bite-sized Crash Coure videos walk you through the 8-step MANIFEST Method, and the in-depth workbook helps you apply the method to whatever you're manifesting.

The best part is, you can use this process over and over again with EVERYTHING—including those manifestations that seem crazy big or even a little like a pipe dream.

When you have a process to use, you get to bypass allll of the mistakes and missteps most people make when they're trying to intentionally manifest what they want.

Which means you'll be able to get what you want (or something even better) a whole lot faster.

Sound good?

>> Learn more about the MANIFEST Method Crash Course here: www.jenniferblanchard.net/crashcourse

PLEASE LEAVE A REVIEW ON AMAZON

Dear Reader,

I just wanted to say **thank you so much for reading and supporting this book.** *Manifest Everything* is the book I wish someone had handed to me back in 2008 when I first watched the movie, *The Secret*, and learned about the Law of Attraction and that I could co-create my life with the Universe and get anything I wanted. I know it's going to be a huge help for you, wherever you are on your intentional manifesting journey.

As an independent, self-published author, it really helps me spread the word and get this book into more hands when you leave a five-star review (only if you loved the book, of course!)

So if you could **please head over to:** www.manifesteverythingbook.com (this link goes directly to the book's Amazon page) **and leave me a five-star review**, it would mean the world to me.

Dream life or bust,
Jennifer Blanchard

ACKNOWLEDGMENTS

Thank you to my readers—new and returning—for picking up this book, reading it, using it, and (hopefully!) loving it.

Thank you to my boyfriend, Dave, for being the best evidence ever of the Manifest Method's effectiveness.

Thank you to my longtime friend and editor, Mary DeRosa. Without you I couldn't do what I do as well as I do it.

Thank you to Alisa Divine, my author life partner-in-crime, friend and the best accountability buddy. This book wouldn't exist if I didn't have you to share every last insight and thought in my head with.

Thank you to my ACIM Reverend and friend, Barbara Adams. You taught me how to pray in a much more powerful way and it has changed my life forever. And so it is.

Thank you to my family, friends, and online community for the continued love and support. You keep me going when the going gets tough.

And thank you to my faves and those whose work in the world has been a part of my spiritual journey: Mike Dooley, Abraham-Hicks, Neville Goddard, Bob Proctor, Brad Yates, Dr. Joe Dispenza, Neale Donald Walsh, *A Course In Miracles*, Pastor Michael Todd, Amanda Frances, Katrina Ruth, and so many others. Whether named or unnamed (mostly because I'm terrible at remembering names), I thank you.

ABOUT THE AUTHOR

Jennifer Blanchard is the self-made bestselling author of *F*ck the How*, *Quantum Leap Your Life*, and *Manifest Everything*, which are roadmaps for manifesting your dreams and desires without needing to know the How ahead of time.

Her practical approach to intentional manifesting is doable and easy to understand. Readers of her books and students of her courses have said Jennifer clarifies and expands on everything they've previously learned about manifestation.

She has a Bachelor's degree in Journalism and Public Relations with a minor in Creative Writing.

Jennifer has authored more than a dozen books, including several works of fiction, and is co-author of the book, *Miraclefesting: Inspiring Stories to Help You Recognize and Create Everyday Miracles In Your Life*.

- facebook.com/thefeelgoodlife
- instagram.com/thefeelgoodlife
- youtube.com/jenniferblanchard
- amazon.com/stores/Jennifer-Blanchard/author/B091RH6JCR
- tiktok.com/@fuckthehow

Made in the USA
Middletown, DE
23 July 2024